30 Writing Prompts 30 Books
Let The Journey Begin
By
Marier Farley

Acknowledgement
I would like to thank F. H. Blocker, S. N. Patterson, D. J. Patterson II, V. Z. H. Hughes, K. J. and N. J. Hughes, V. P. Hughes, Y. R. Hughes, R. E. Hughes, and D. Patterson for helping me get finished with this book. Without your encouragement, I would've stopped writing. Thank you. Special thanks go to my special sister who went on my first date with me at the age of 3 as my chaperone, M. M. D. Hughes. She will always hold a special place in my heart. She died at the age of 4.

Dedication

This book is dedicated to the ladies in green, Lula B Edwards, a beloved aunt and Brenda Joyce Logan Turner Hughes, a beloved sister-in-law. Both of these ladies lost the battle with illness the first to a stroke and the second to bone cancer, but they won the war because they are home with our Lord and Savior Jesus the Christ. I will see you again.

1. He picked up speed as he prepared to make his final run toward home. Suddenly in front of him was an Indian encampment. His mind cannot wrap itself around this fact, and he kept riding. His horse knew this was the final stretch and moved even faster. He passed each teepee with increasing speed. Suddenly a child ran out in front of him. His time spent training with his father riding for speed, grabbing a lamb came into play, and he leaned down and grabbed the child so his course would not trample her. Leaning down causes the arrow meant for his heart to sail harmlessly over his head. A woman runs out with her arms outstretched and he dropped the girl into them and kept riding. He did not slow down until the town came into view although he knew he had left his pursuers far behind and they were no longer chasing him.

Complete the story. What happened before this incident? Why was the encampment there? What happened after the incident? This story should be approximately 30,000 words.

2. The song seemed to go on forever. It only lasted five minutes. But those were the longest five minutes of his life. He could not believe the lady singing the song was standing right in front of him. The words tore at his heart and made him want to run from the building. But he could not he just stood there allowing the words to wash over him.

Complete the story. Did he just lose someone close? What happened? Why did the song affect him? What was he doing before the song started? Who was the woman? This story should be approximately 30,000-words. Be sure to add humor and several plot twist as you develop the story.

3. Sydney was walking in front of her home with an orange reflective vest on her back. Suddenly a gray SUV rolled up and hit her and kept going. Her son was looking out the window and saw the incident. He called 911, and they responded. The crowd gathered watching as they loaded Sydney into an ambulance. A preteen boy walked up to the policeman and asked him did he know how to use his gun. The policeman was shocked that he answered and said yes. The preteen said you might as well shoot because I am the one that hit that lady. My dad is going to kill me and I would rather you do it than him. The policeman walked the young man to his police car and took him home. They walked to the backyard where the father was cutting grass. When the father looked up and saw the two of them, he turned the machine off and started walking toward them. A silent tear had run down his face before he got them.

What happened next? Why did the preteen have the car? Why was the quality crying? Why did the preteen didn't need his father killed him? What did the police officer say? This prompt should be a 20,000-word story.

4. A man awakens and is very cold. He shouts to his wife. He gets up and begins adding wood to the fire and shouts again for his wife. She does not answer. He stomps around the house and finally goes upstairs. As he nears the top of the steps, he notices how cold it is. Suddenly he remembers that he sent his wife and two children upstairs away from the fire because he was angry because he got fired. As he enters the room, he sees his wife and children huddled together under a thin quilt. As he gets closer, he sees they are barely breathing. He picks all three of them up and takes them downstairs.

What happens next? What happened before? Why did he get fired? Is this his first wife or his second? Are these her children or stepchildren? Complete this story. This prompt should be at these 40,000-words.

5. Write a story about compromising your
    beliefs in the face of your peers. This
    prompt should be 30,000-words and
    have a strong conflict and conclusion.
    Be sure to give problems and solutions
    as you go about developing the
    story.(Nonfiction)

6. Three people are sitting in jazz bar at an upscale hotel. Two men and one lady. The lady is on the end, and the middle guy opens a package and asks her to squeeze it. Three immediately leave, the lady and one guy catch the elevator while the other one goes outside. The pair are friends and turning into lovers. They share a kiss on the elevator and get off one floor below where they should and immediately go into an empty room undress and scan their clothes. They find several bugs and the guy gives her a change of clothes while he dons a new set. They scan again and find that they have one bug somewhere. She hands him the device they were supposed to secure and make their way to the adjoining room. He puts the device in a protected box just before stepping into the other room. The device has special capabilities. As soon as it is hidden, it figures out how to send a signal.

What happens next? This prompt can be a romantic suspense story with a strong story line that includes several plot twist that will cause the reader to believe they know the end. The ending should be a shocker. This prompt can also be a slight cliffhanger that will lead to a series of books.

7. A 60-year-old Mattapan Massachusetts detective meets and marries a 56-year-old woman. He has worked the case of the Mattapan killer and with her help solved it. They adopt a dog. His chief ask him to work three more years. His wife Angela is a wedding planner, and she thinks that's fine.

What is the next case? How does he solve it? Does Angela help? What happens in their domestic life? This prompt should be a 50,000-word story that is a series starter. Several plot twist that elude to more books in this series.

8. He left the card game in the middle of a
    winning streak and went home. His
    buddies were angry with him, but he
    had to leave. When he got home, it was
    ransacked, and his wife was sitting in
    the middle of the bed with a gun
    pointed at the door.
What happened? Are there clues? Is this
something that is related to his life or her
life? This prompt should be a 30,000-word
story with a strong romantic twist.

9. What is reconciliation? How does it
    work? When should it be considered?
    Answer these and pose other questions
    to turn this into a 25,000-word book. If
    enough research is completed, turn it
    into a 40,000-word book.

10. You've been given one-time access to a time machine to visit your younger self. After a brief pause, you know the when and the where, hop in the machine and take off. When there, you chat with your younger self but offer one piece of advice to him/her that you hope will change his/her future for the better. Start with your arrival in the time machine (and what does your time machine look like) and end with your arrival in the future noticing something that has changed.

This should be a 50,000-word story with a strong romantic interest.

11. "I'd love to _____ but my _____ just _____!" I can't _____ it happened but it was _____ that something was _____. (And then write a story that follows it.)

This prompt is a 2000-word story with a moral.

12. Write a story that begins with the title of the book you've most recently read. Include characters from some other story you have written. Combine them to make a romantic suspense story that leads to several dramatic scenes that cause problems for the couple. Allow the heroine to be the one who puts her foot in her mouth that causes some of the problems.

This prompt should be a 30,000 or 40,000-word story.

13. After a long, hard day of work, you return home—the only problem is, your front door is wide open, all your lights are on, and there's a sword stuck in the ceiling. The rest of your house looks normal, but you also notice several holes dug in your backyard. What's going on?

This prompt should be the 40,000-story with a strong romantic interest.

14. With a book deadline fast approaching and an empty document tormenting you on your laptop, you realize you need a change of scenery to get your work done. You go to the airport and take the next flight out. Your travels take you to the gorgeous country of Ireland. But now you need a place to stay. You find your way to a quaint local bed and breakfast: the perfect place to write. Only problem? The attractive owner of the B&B can't take her eyes off of you! Is this the beginning of a new romance, or maybe just the material you needed for your book? Is she a fae? Are you somehow enchanted and transported to a different plane of existence?

This prompt should be a 40,000-word book with a strong romantic interest and suspense. It can be paranormal.

15. Praying Throughout the Day. This prompt should be an inspirational book to help people expand their praying. You could make it something like 365 things to pray for during the year or something like that. You must use your imagination. (Nonfiction)

16. You have to start compromising yourself or your morals for the people around you then it is probably time to change the people around. (Fiction)

This prompt should be a 30,000 to 50,000-word story with suspense and a strong romantic interest. Include humor throughout the story. Also give the secondary characters a romantic happily ever after.

17.-18. Two men headed to work dressed in nice suits and driving nice cars. They pass a broken down vehicle. Both men and stop to offer assistance. The first one goes into his trunk and pulls out bottled water and hands it to a family sitting on the side of the road. He then hands the mother a $20 bill and drives off. The second **guy** drives off. He returns 30 minutes later with a creeper, a set of tools, food for the family, and a set of overalls for the guy who is trying to repair the car.

This prompt should be two stories each told from the perspective of the men stopped. Each story should be 30,000 words. What is the back story? Is the guy repairing the car the same race as the man stopped? Does the guy who returned remain until the car is repaired? Does the second guy return after work?

19. You are a 40-year old man who lost his job six months ago. Your wife died three years ago of cancer. You have no children. Your home will go into foreclosure soon. All your friends seem to have disappeared. You sit on a bench in the park and let the sunshine smile on you. Your despair is evident. Suddenly a lady sits next to you and hands you a card that says "Try Jesus." What do you do? What is the back story?

This prompt should be a 50,000-word story with a strong romantic interest. Relate several conflicts that led to not only his firing but what he does to solve his moral dilemmas.

20. Two seventy-year-olds get married. They have fifteen grandchildren between them. They were high school sweethearts. One is retired military, and the other is retired law enforcement. They lost touch when each went to a different college.

What is the story? This prompt should be a 50,000-word story with at least three strong romantic interest. There should also be suspense and action included.

21. A group of church campers get lost on a day trip and hold up in a cave. Two of them sneak away during the night and get lost.

Why did they sneak away? What is the back story about the trip? Are the two part of the group or are they invited, guest? This prompt should be a 50,000-word story with a strong love interest and several plot twist.

21. We as servant leaders of this church
with the help of the Lord will fulfill our
mission of being men of character
commitment and compassion. You read
this statement as you look at ten men in
front of the church.
What's story of these ten men? Are they
deacons? Are they trustees? Is this an
initiation ceremony? What type of church
is it? This prompt should be a 40,000-word
story. It can include a strong romantic
interest and must be Christian based.

22. You just finished reading a story, and a line keeps running through your head. "If you are finished panicking, John and I are praying. We're not lost; we just can't see the path. But God can." Now you are on your life journey. You have success, a nice home, lots of so-called friends, but you feel lost. How do you find your way?

This prompt should be a 30,000-word story. It should be Christian based and include a strong romantic interest. What is the back story? Is this your life story or someone else's?

23. You just landed yourself in the middle
of a dispute with a competitor who has
accused you of sending a spy to their
company. The person they are talking
about is not only a former employee
but also a former love interest. She
walked away because you spent too
much time building your company and
not enough time on her. She is self-
centered. As you listen to your team of
lawyers and company executives talk a
line your pastor said in a sermon many
months ago roll into your head. "This
did not catch God by surprise."
How does this make you feel? Write the
story from three points of view. Include
humor as well as a strong moral. This
prompt should be a 50,000-word story
with a strong romantic interest, intrigue,
betrayal, and love lost then found.

24.-27. You are a 32-year-old woman almost 300 pounds overweight with seven children all under the age of 6. You are married to a very successful well-toned man who runs 5 miles every evening. You are having a discussion after the kids have gone to their rooms and you tell your husband that you want to have weight loss surgery. He looks at you and says you have too much time on your hands and since you do perhaps it is time you got pregnant again. He then tells you to wash your hair because you have baby gunk in it and leaves to run. You know that he means to have sex when he returns. You go to the bathroom and turn the shower on then proceed to call a lawyer and talk to him while the water is running because you believe your husband has cameras and recording equipment throughout the house. You explain what happened tonight and other details such as the fact that you have to submit your grocery list to his secretary and he erase what he thinks you should not have. He gives you small amounts of money and a gas card. You have the finest of everything that he likes. You want out. You then say to the lawyer. Are you a friend of my husband? His reply is that they are golfing buddies. You say okay. If they find your body, then he is responsible and hangs up. The lawyer tells his security chief that his newest client needs hidden protection and explains that this will be pro bono work.

This prompt should be a 50,000 to 60,000-word story with a strong romantic interest, suspense, and several plot twist. The bodyguard should play a prominent role in this. Write it with him as the hero. Write another version with the lawyer as the hero. The woman should be the heroine. Write another version where the husband is the hero.

28. You are a 37-year-old woman who has only to defend your dissertation before getting your doctorate in psychology. You have had several failed romantic encounters because they refused to see you as the strong woman that you are. They wanted to mold you into what they wanted. As you walk into the conference room to make your defense, you notice a chair is empty. The chairman looks at you and smiles then says, "We have a slight change of the group. Dr. Jones had a heart attack, but we did not want to hold you up since we know you have already accepted a position contingent upon you receiving your degree this semester. The door opens behind you and you hear a familiar walk enter the room. It is the one guy that you can't stop remembering. You know his walk because he always wore cowboy boots even with his tailored suits. He walks past you and takes the empty seat.

What happens next? What is the back story? Does she get her degree or does he derail her? This prompt should be a 50,000-word story with a strong romantic interest. Do the research on what it takes to become a doctoral student in psychology and what it takes to get the degree. Don't let the story end with the degree or non-degree. What happens afterward?

29. You are a new student to the college you have wanted to attend since you were twelve years old. But everyone around you is so young that you feel like a grandfather. You are thirty years old. A car accident that killed your parents and injured your brother have gotten in the way of you getting the degree you wanted. Your chance has finally come. What degree are you pursuing? What happened after the accident? Where is your brother? How do you handle the age difference? Do you meet someone to love? Do you drop out because of the pressure? This prompt should be a Christian based story with several moral dilemmas included. How does faith help this story along? This prompt should be a 50,000-word story with a strong romantic interest.

30. You are a 36-year-old single mother of three kids. The 12-year old has become rebellious, the nine-year-old withdrawn and the two-year-old is just in his terrible twos. Your husband died two days before he was to return on his last deployment. You work as a civilian on the military base so your circumstances in housing change. Your husband's commander is also single. His wife died during childbirth, and his 13-year-old daughter was raised by her grandparents since he could not be released from his duty. He is planning on retiring and has been helping you out with various things.

How does this story play out? Is she close to her parents? Are her dead husband's parent's part of their lives? What is the story between the two central characters or does another character come in to be the hero? This prompt should be a Christian based romance with lots of twists but not suspense. It should work into a 50,000-word story. Complete research on army housing of civilians, teen rebellion and the issue with the middle child. Also, blended families if you are going to blend the families. Be sure to add humor throughout the story.

About the Author

Karen has been a reader from the age of 4. For her young adult life, she would always be seen with a book or asking someone to read to her. She began to write stories in the first grade and has not stopped writing since. She has ventured into many different areas in her life before finally settling on writing short stories after retiring from 37 years in the public school system. She has traveled extensively throughout the continent of North America. You may friend her on Facebook. She writes under the name Marier Farley as well
She has several other eBooks as well as several other books that are coming out soon.

Stranger In Town

To Love Wisely

Twice Shy

A Father For Me, Meghan

They Knew How To Cook

It's Time to Move

Praying Prayers of Accountability

Praying the Promises of God

Praying Prayers of Encouragement

Prayers of Gratitude

Prayer Changes Things

Prayers For Relationship Building

www.ingramcontent.com/pod-product-compliance
Lightning Source LLC
LaVergne TN
LVHW020059190726
843498LV00012B/1897